Hkya

D1105738

GREAT ESCAPES OF WORLD WAR II

OUTRUNNING
THE NAZIS

THE BRAVE ESCAPE OF RESISTANCE FIGHTER SVEN SOMME

by Matt Chandler

CAPSTONE PRESS
a capstone imprint

Graphic Library is published by Capstone Press,
1710 Roe Crest Drive, North Mankato, Minnesota 56003
www.mycapstone.com

Library of Congress Cataloging-in-Publication data is available on the Library of Congress website.
ISBN 978-1-5157-3529-8 (library binding)
ISBN 978-1-5157-3534-2 (paperback)
ISBN 978-1-5157-3546-5 (eBook PDF)

Editor
Anna Butzer

Art Director
Nathan Gassman

Designer
Ted Williams

Media Researcher
Wanda Winch

Production Specialist
Gene Bentdahl

Cover Illustrator
Pericles Junior

Illustrator
Daniele Nicotra

Colorist
Douglas A. Sirois

Design Element: Shutterstock: aodaodaodaod, paper texture,esfera,
map design, Natalya Kalyatina, barbed wire design)

Printed and bound in the United States of America.
10042S17

TABLE OF CONTENTS

THE RESISTANCE

B y 1944 World War II (1939–1945) had claimed millions of lives and devastated much of Europe. But after five bloody years of war, the American and British-led Allied forces had gained the upper hand over the German-led Axis Powers. Their success was due, in part, to the support received by resistance fighters. These volunteers supported the Allied forces. They assisted in many ways. Resistance fighters sheltered pilots shot down in enemy territory. They offered medical assistance and helped the men escape to safety. And, in many cases, the resistance members worked as spies, gathering valuable information.

Unlike soldiers, the resistance fighters were just regular people. They didn't have special training, and they weren't always the best men and women for the job. They just had a passion to protect their land and end the Nazi occupation of their countries.

Sven Somme was one of thousands of members of the resistance aiding in the defeat of the Nazis. He worked as a resistance spy, secretly photographing Nazi war boats and troops behind enemy lines. Somme didn't come from a military background. He was a zoologist from a tiny town in Norway. Three of Somme's siblings were also in the resistance, but it is the story of Sven Somme that is so gripping. How does a man of no special skills or physical strengths outwit the Nazis? How does he selflessly aid the Allies, escape a death sentence, and travel 200 miles to freedom?

RUN TO FREEDOM

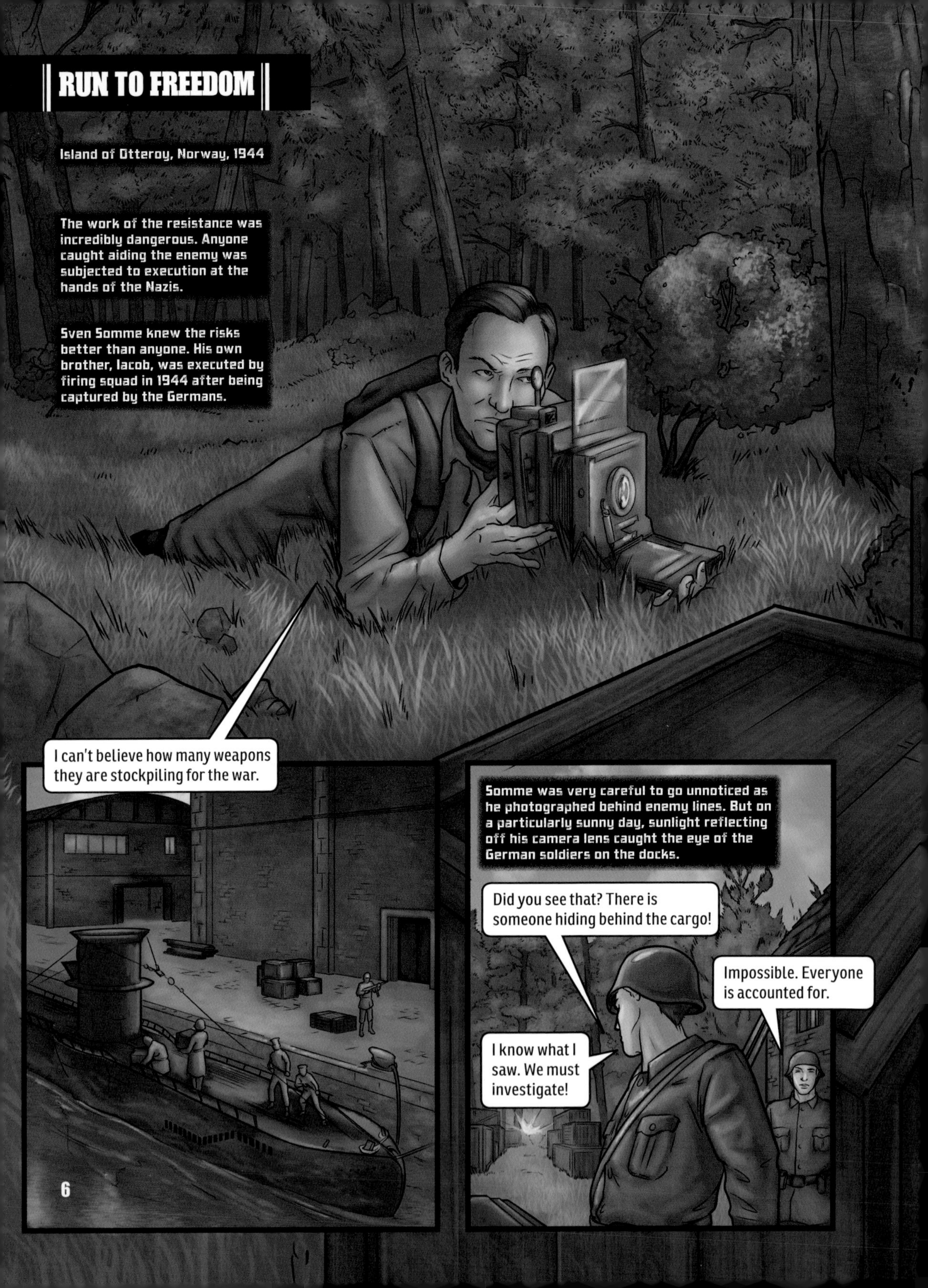
Island of Otteroy, Norway, 1944
The work of the resistance was incredibly dangerous. Anyone caught aiding the enemy was subjected to execution at the hands of the Nazis.
Sven Somme knew the risks better than anyone. His own brother, Iacob, was executed by firing squad in 1944 after being captured by the Germans.
I can't believe how many weapons they are stockpiling for the war.
Somme was very careful to go unnoticed as he photographed behind enemy lines. But on a particularly sunny day, sunlight reflecting off his camera lens caught the eye of the German soldiers on the docks.
Did you see that? There is someone hiding behind the cargo!
Impossible. Everyone is accounted for.
I know what I saw. We must investigate!

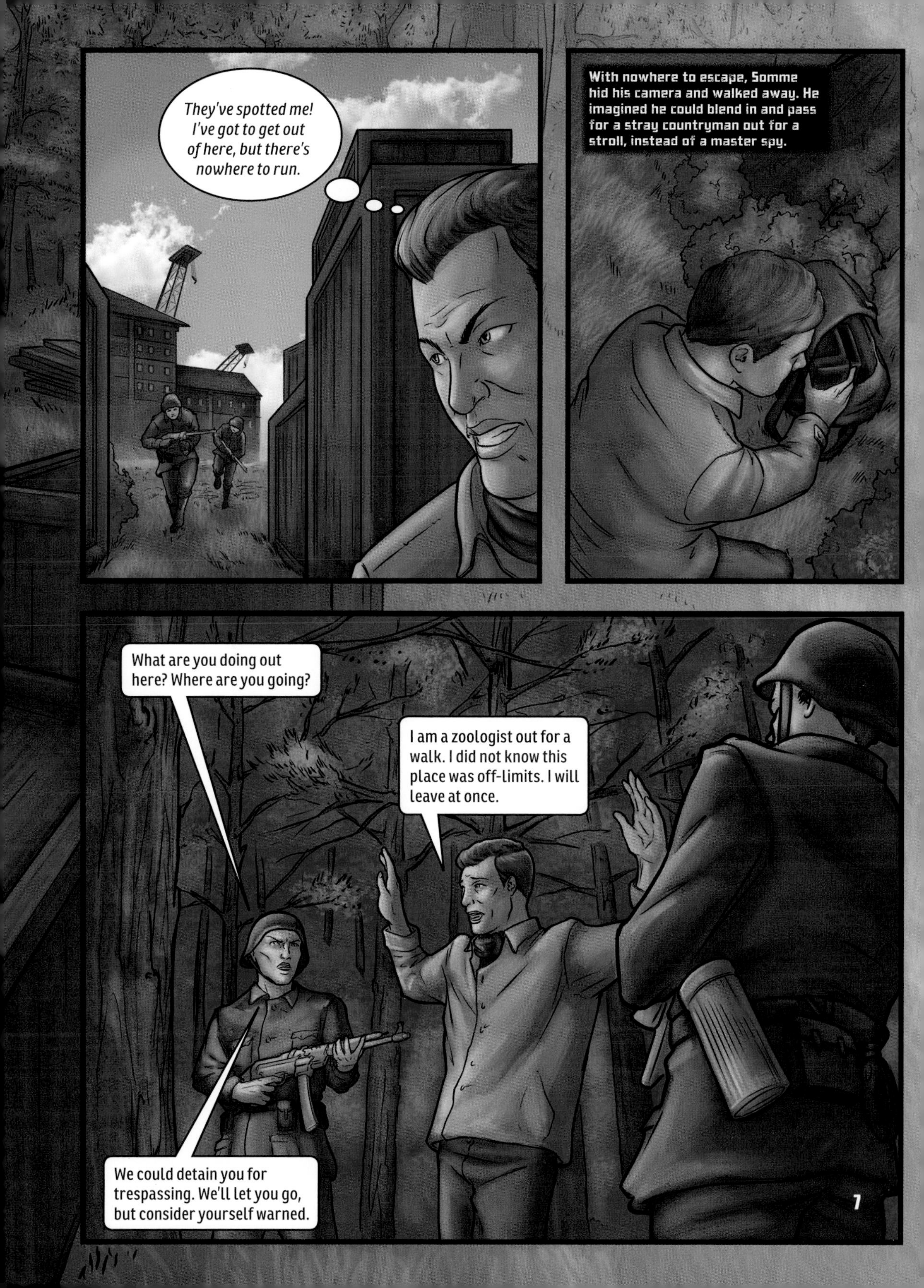
They've spotted me! I've got to get out of here, but there's nowhere to run.
With nowhere to escape, Somme hid his camera and walked away. He imagined he could blend in and pass for a stray countryman out for a stroll, instead of a master spy.
What are you doing out here? Where are you going?
I am a zoologist out for a walk. I did not know this place was off-limits. I will leave at once.
We could detain you for trespassing. We'll let you go, but consider yourself warned.

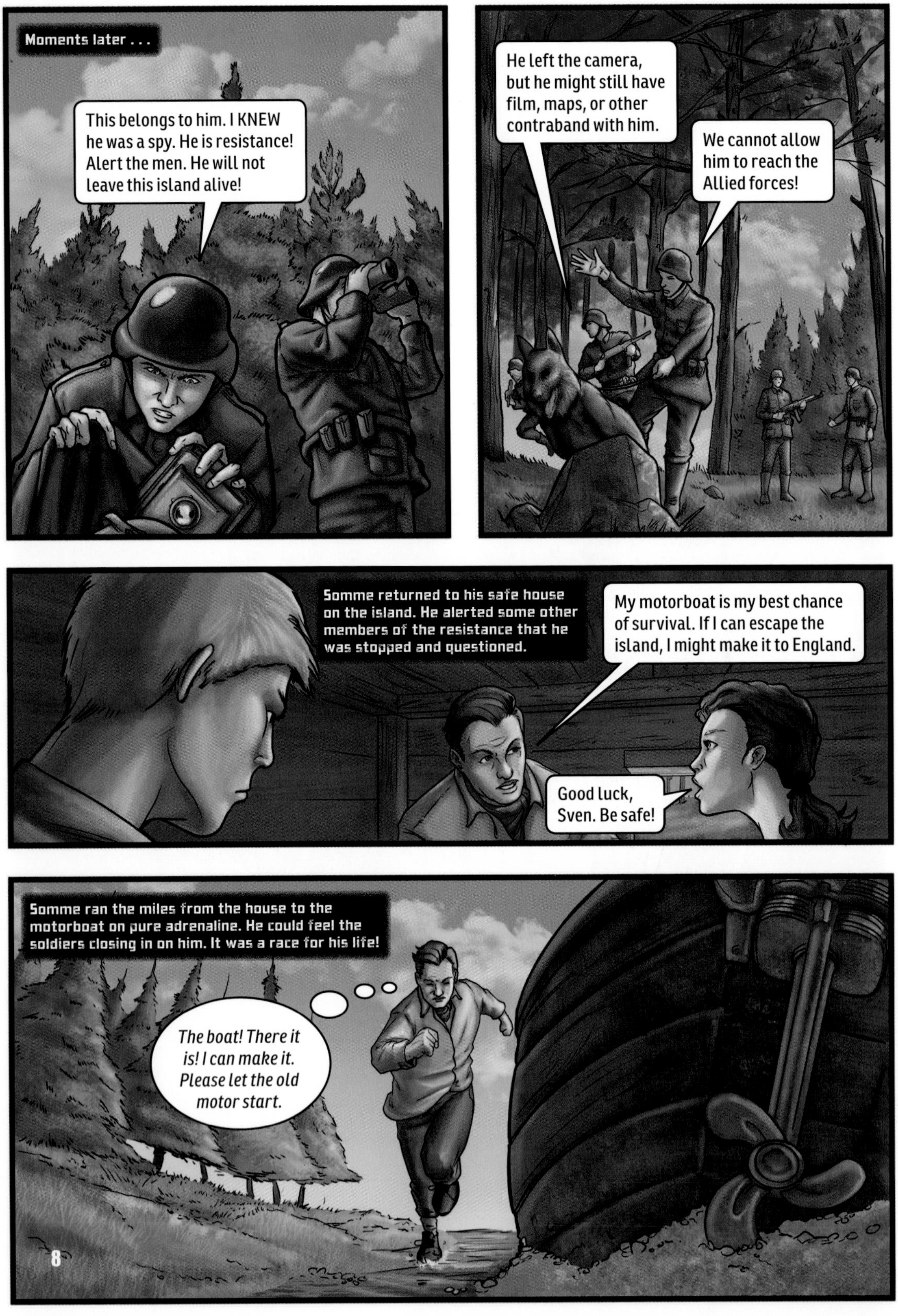
Moments later . . .
This belongs to him. I KNEW he was a spy. He is resistance! Alert the men. He will not leave this island alive!
He left the camera, but he might still have film, maps, or other contraband with him.
We cannot allow him to reach the Allied forces!
Somme returned to his safe house on the island. He alerted some other members of the resistance that he was stopped and questioned.
My motorboat is my best chance of survival. If I can escape the island, I might make it to England.
Good luck, Sven. Be safe!
Somme ran the miles from the house to the motorboat on pure adrenaline. He could feel the soldiers closing in on him. It was a race for his life!
The boat! There it is! I can make it. Please let the old motor start.

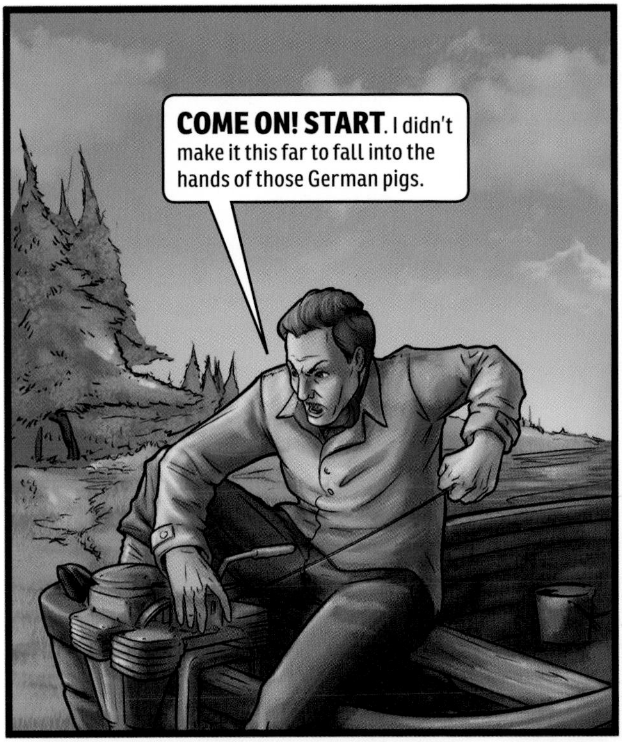
COME ON! START. I didn't make it this far to fall into the hands of those German pigs.

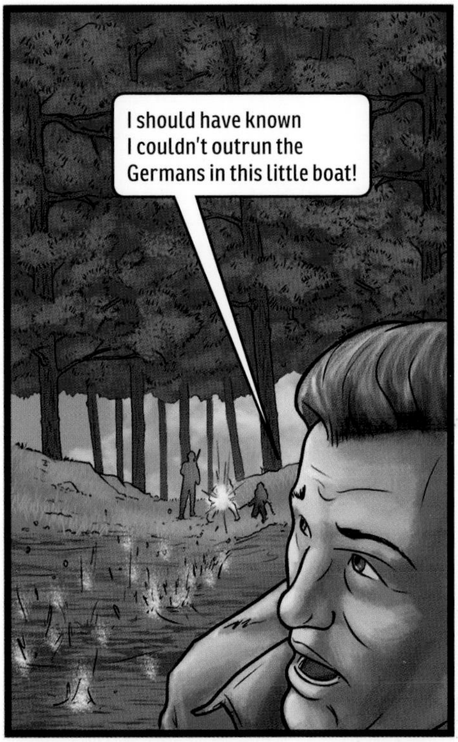
I should have known I couldn't outrun the Germans in this little boat!

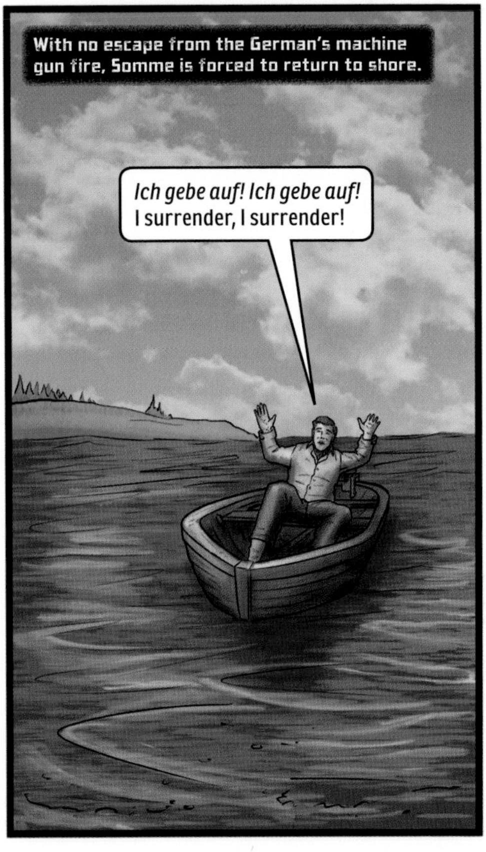
With no escape from the German's machine gun fire, Somme is forced to return to shore.
Ich gebe auf! Ich gebe auf! I surrender, I surrender!

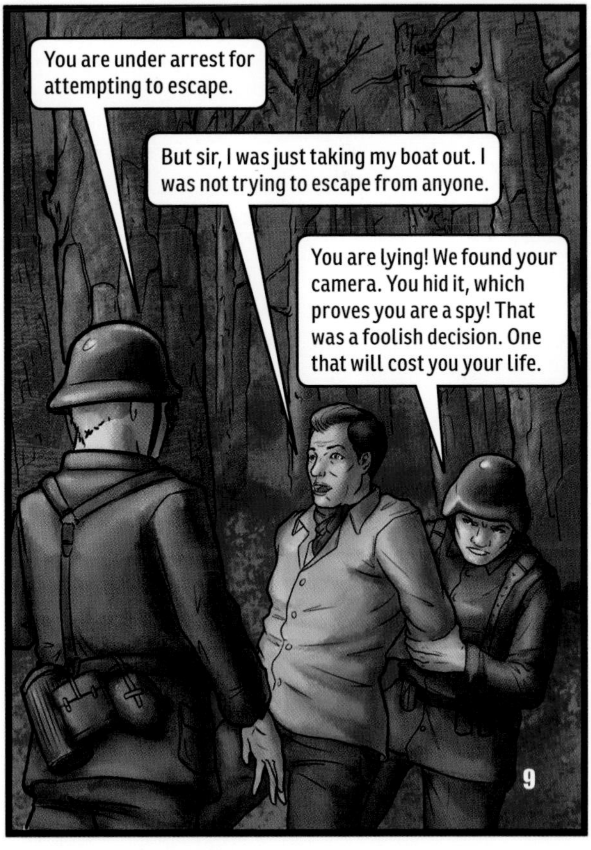
You are under arrest for attempting to escape.
But sir, I was just taking my boat out. I was not trying to escape from anyone.
You are lying! We found your camera. You hid it, which proves you are a spy! That was a foolish decision. One that will cost you your life.

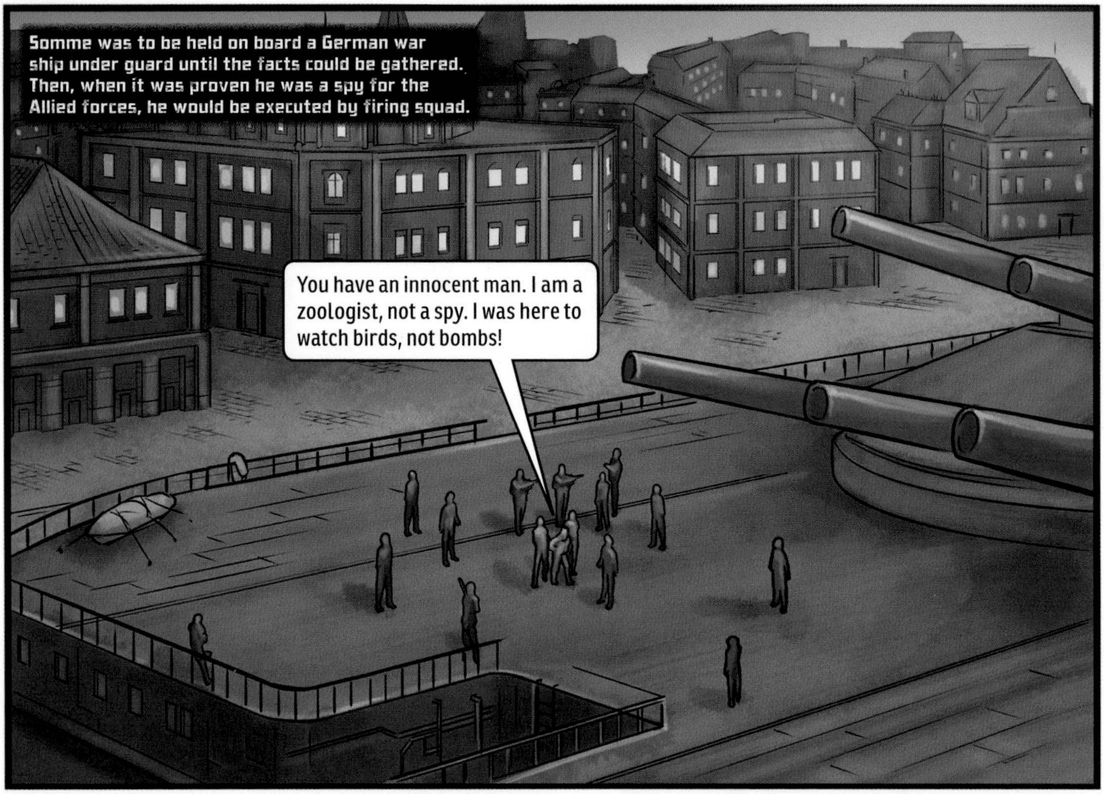
Somme was to be held on board a German war ship under guard until the facts could be gathered. Then, when it was proven he was a spy for the Allied forces, he would be executed by firing squad.
You have an innocent man. I am a zoologist, not a spy. I was here to watch birds, not bombs!

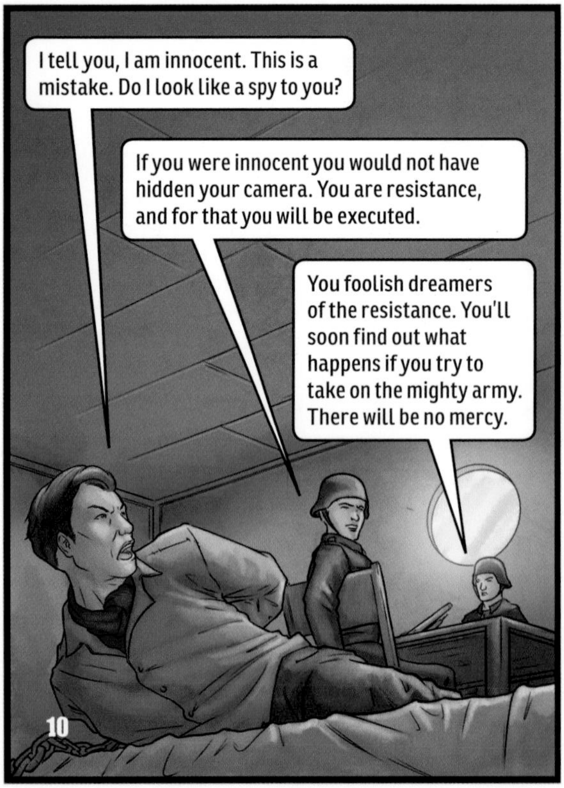
I tell you, I am innocent. This is a mistake. Do I look like a spy to you?
If you were innocent you would not have hidden your camera. You are resistance, and for that you will be executed.
You foolish dreamers of the resistance. You'll soon find out what happens if you try to take on the mighty army. There will be no mercy.

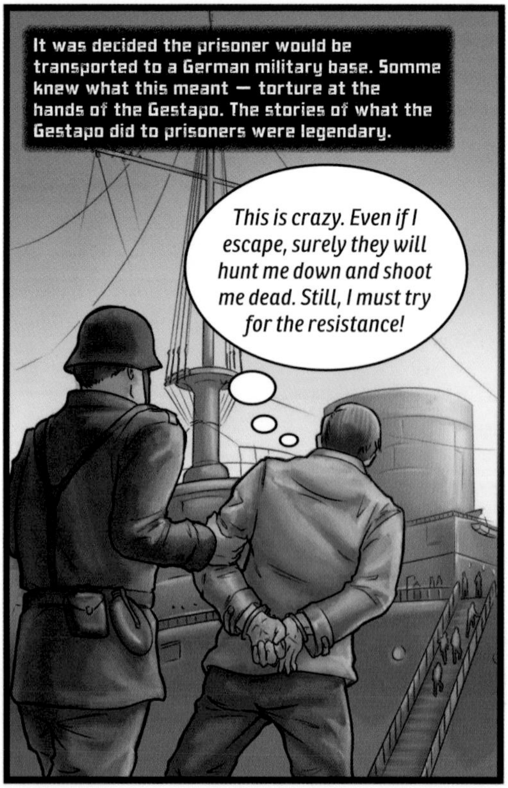
It was decided the prisoner would be transported to a German military base. Somme knew what this meant — torture at the hands of the Gestapo. The stories of what the Gestapo did to prisoners were legendary.
This is crazy. Even if I escape, surely they will hunt me down and shoot me dead. Still, I must try for the resistance!

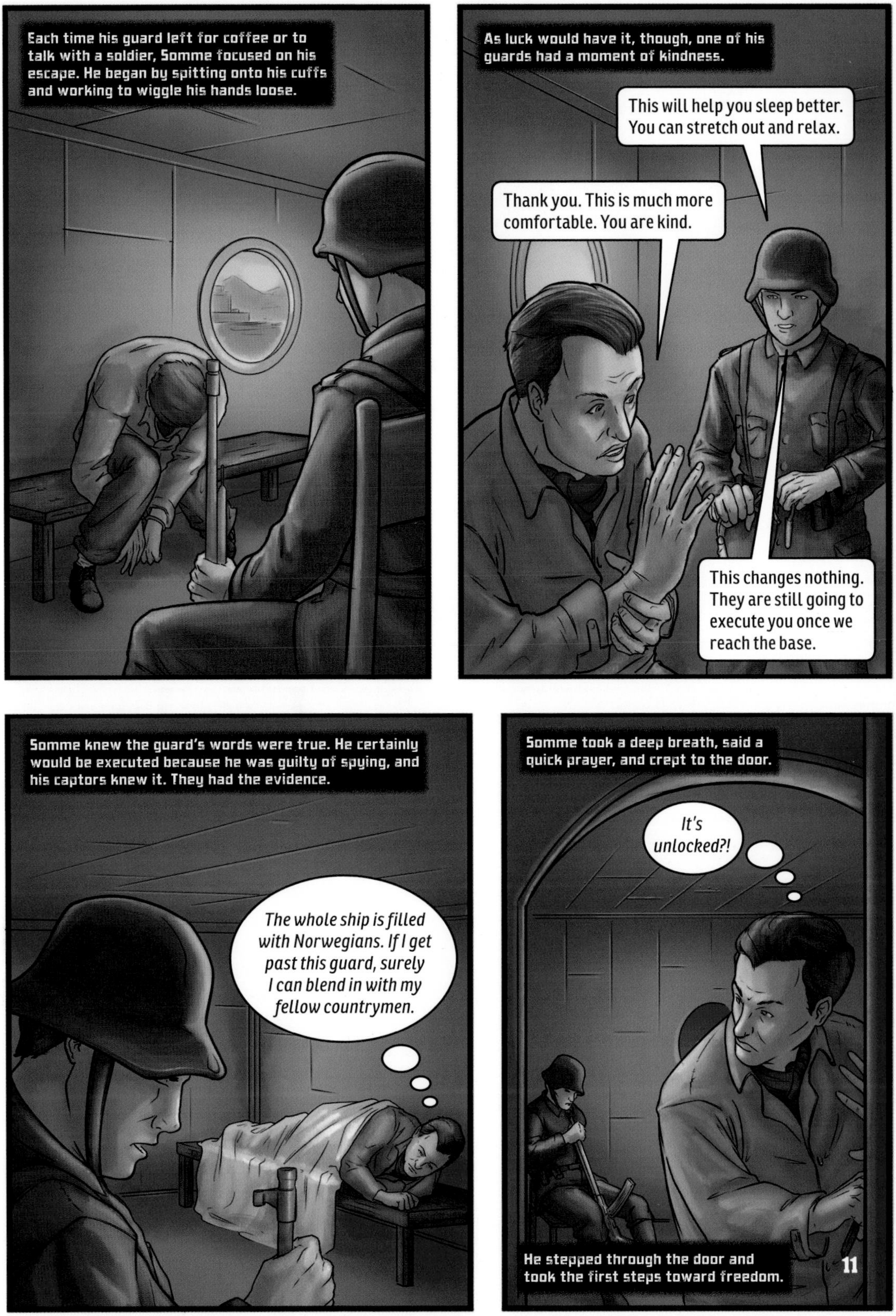
Each time his guard left for coffee or to talk with a soldier, Somme focused on his escape. He began by spitting onto his cuffs and working to wiggle his hands loose.
As luck would have it, though, one of his guards had a moment of kindness.
This will help you sleep better. You can stretch out and relax.
Thank you. This is much more comfortable. You are kind.
This changes nothing. They are still going to execute you once we reach the base.
Somme knew the guard's words were true. He certainly would be executed because he was guilty of spying, and his captors knew it. They had the evidence.
The whole ship is filled with Norwegians. If I get past this guard, surely I can blend in with my fellow countrymen.
Somme took a deep breath, said a quick prayer, and crept to the door.
It's unlocked?!
He stepped through the door and took the first steps toward freedom.

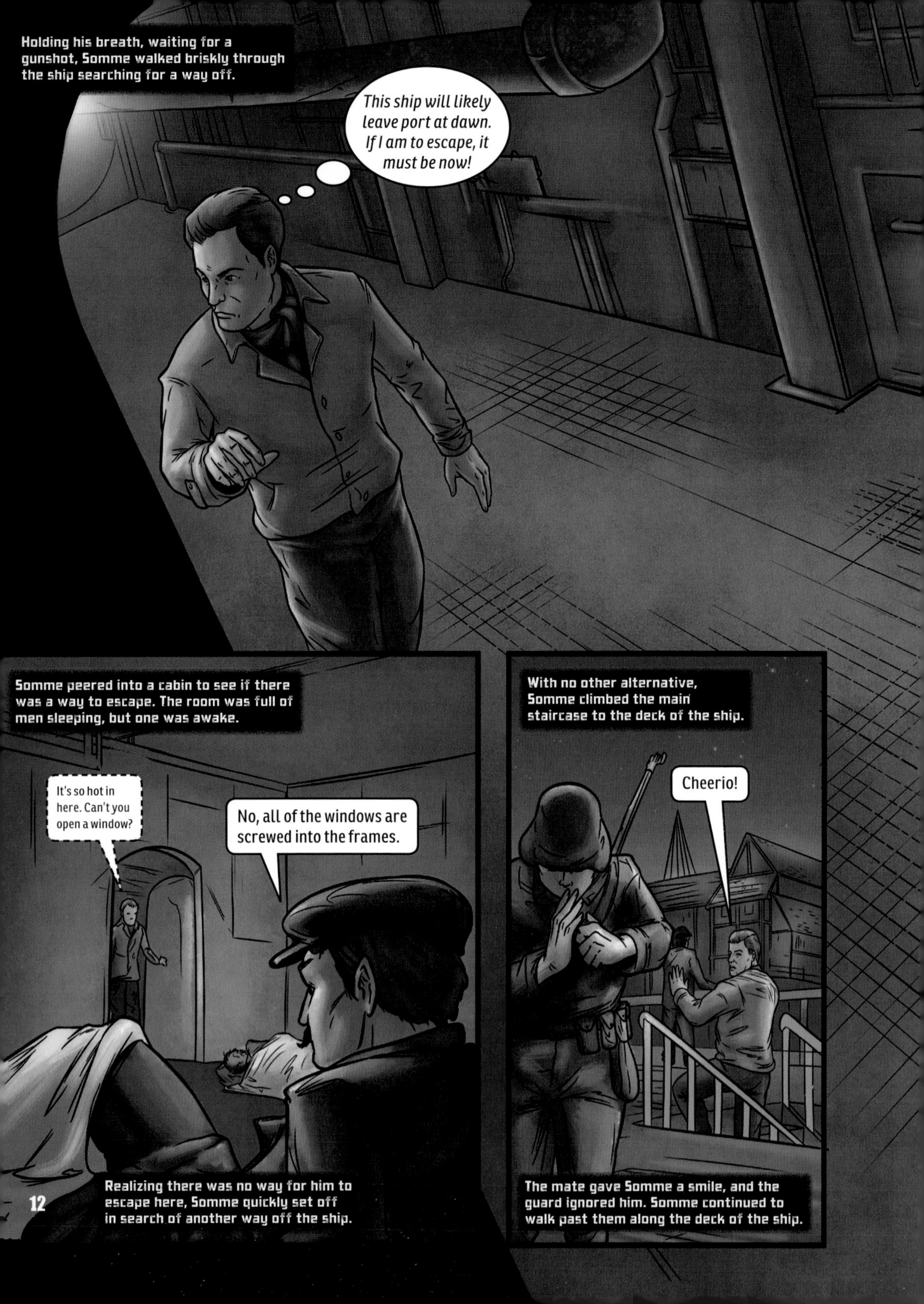
Holding his breath, waiting for a gunshot, Somme walked briskly through the ship searching for a way off.
This ship will likely leave port at dawn. If I am to escape, it must be now!
Somme peered into a cabin to see if there was a way to escape. The room was full of men sleeping, but one was awake.
It's so hot in here. Can't you open a window?
No, all of the windows are screwed into the frames.
Realizing there was no way for him to escape here, Somme quickly set off in search of another way off the ship.
With no other alternative, Somme climbed the main staircase to the deck of the ship.
Cheerio!
The mate gave Somme a smile, and the guard ignored him. Somme continued to walk past them along the deck of the ship.

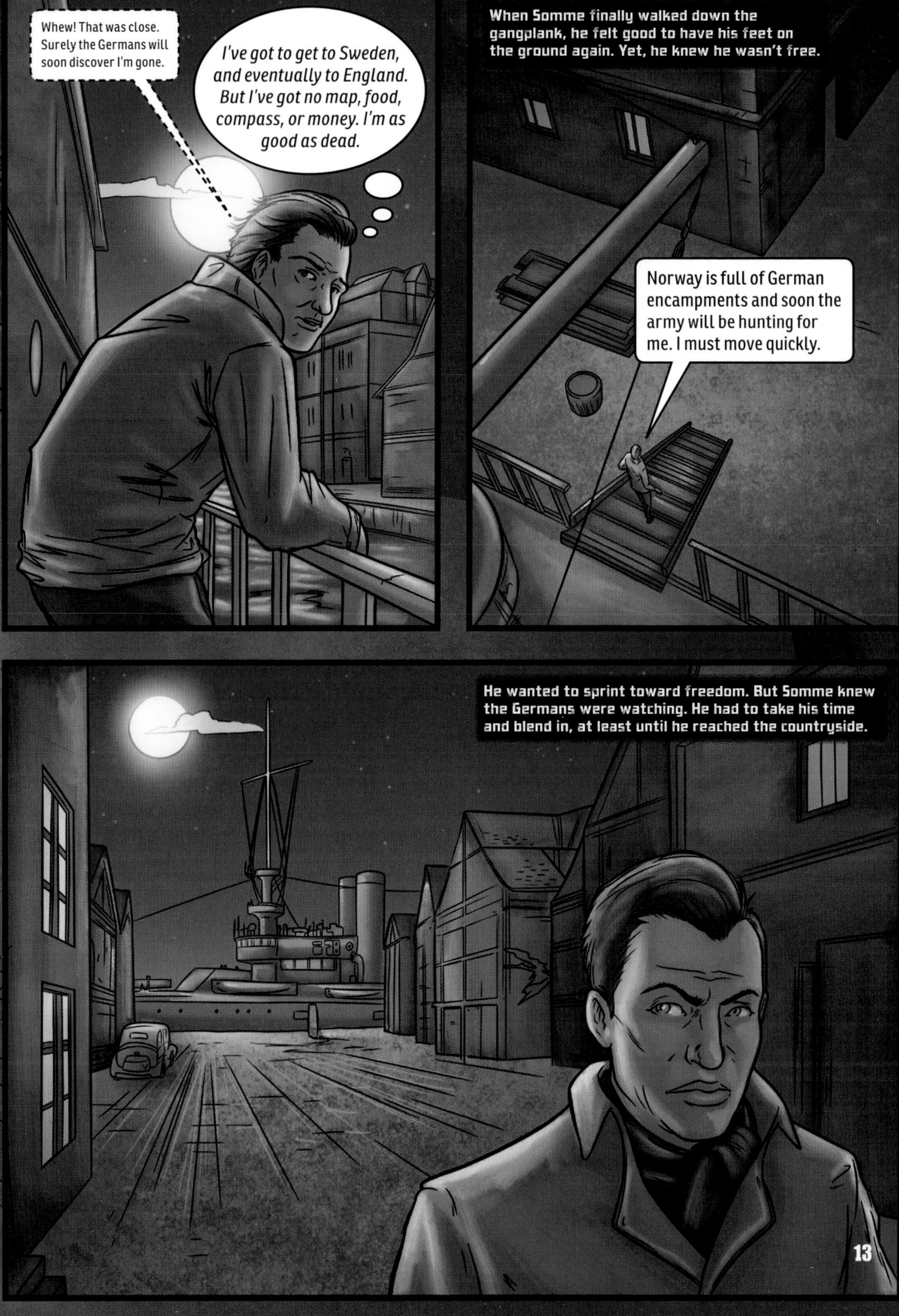
Whew! That was close. Surely the Germans will soon discover I'm gone.
I've got to get to Sweden, and eventually to England. But I've got no map, food, compass, or money. I'm as good as dead.
When Somme finally walked down the gangplank, he felt good to have his feet on the ground again. Yet, he knew he wasn't free.
Norway is full of German encampments and soon the army will be hunting for me. I must move quickly.
He wanted to sprint toward freedom. But Somme knew the Germans were watching. He had to take his time and blend in, at least until he reached the countryside.

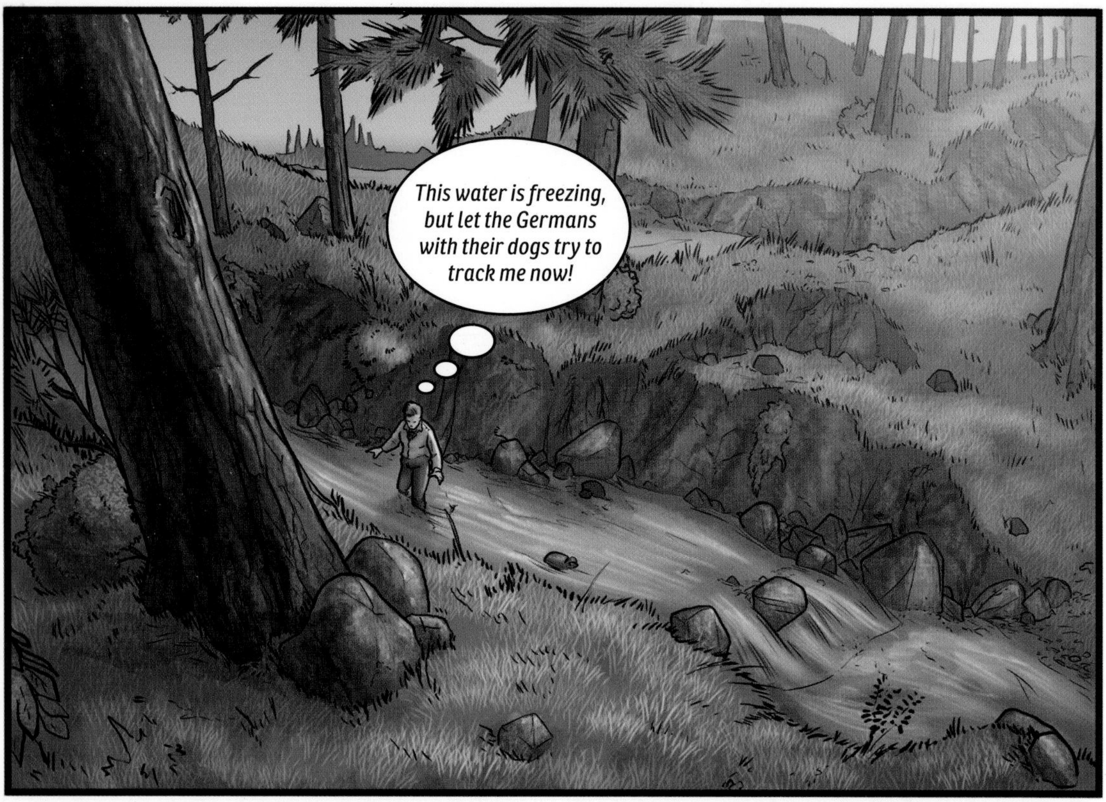
This water is freezing, but let the Germans with their dogs try to track me now!

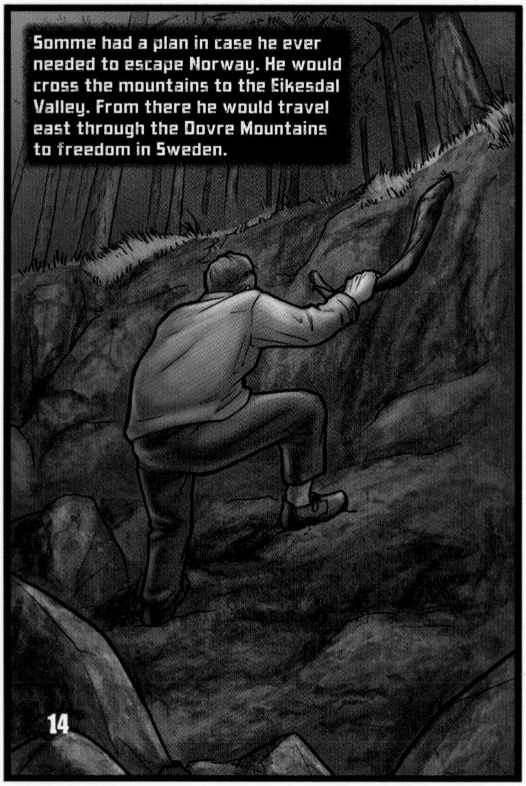
Somme had a plan in case he ever needed to escape Norway. He would cross the mountains to the Eikesdal Valley. From there he would travel east through the Dovre Mountains to freedom in Sweden.

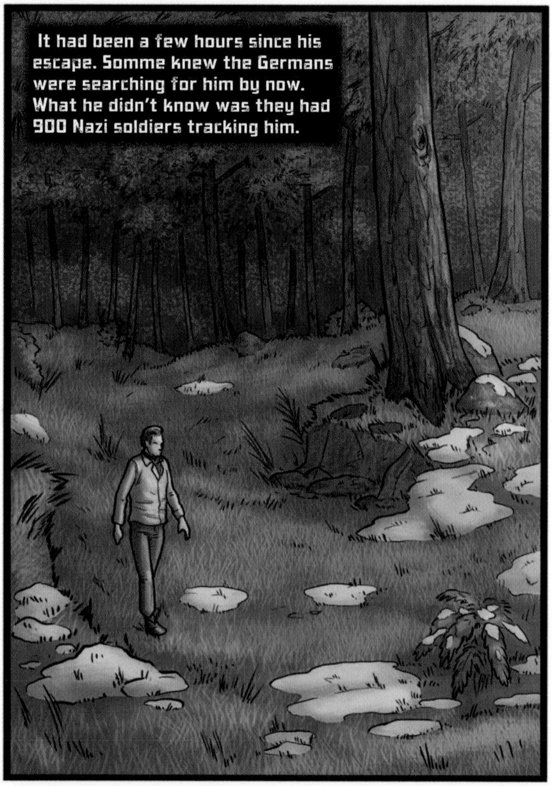
It had been a few hours since his escape. Somme knew the Germans were searching for him by now. What he didn't know was they had 900 Nazi soldiers tracking him.

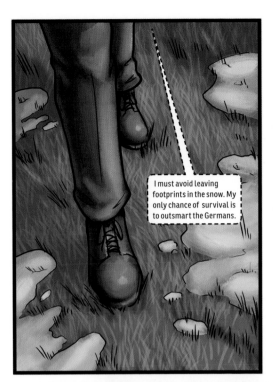

I must avoid leaving footprints in the snow. My only chance of survival is to outsmart the Germans.

My best hope is to hike high into the mountains, but there will be no avoiding the snow. I'll leave a trail for the Germans to track me down!

Then he got an idea . . .

This can work. It MUST work. Just like photographing from the treetops, but instead I must jump between the trees. It is my only hope.

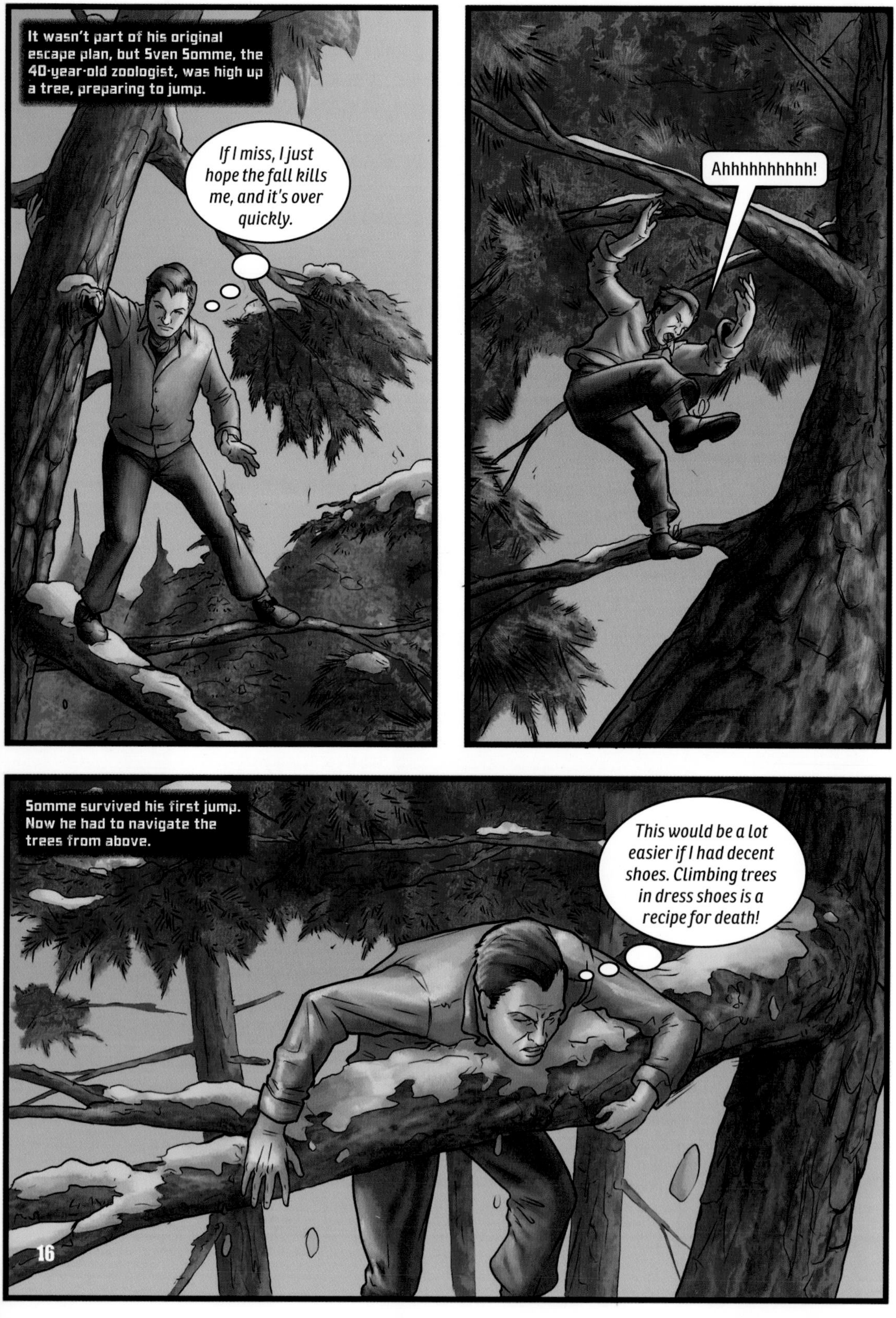
It wasn't part of his original escape plan, but Sven Somme, the 40-year-old zoologist, was high up a tree, preparing to jump.
If I miss, I just hope the fall kills me, and it's over quickly.
Ahhhhhhhhhh!
Somme survived his first jump. Now he had to navigate the trees from above.
This would be a lot easier if I had decent shoes. Climbing trees in dress shoes is a recipe for death!

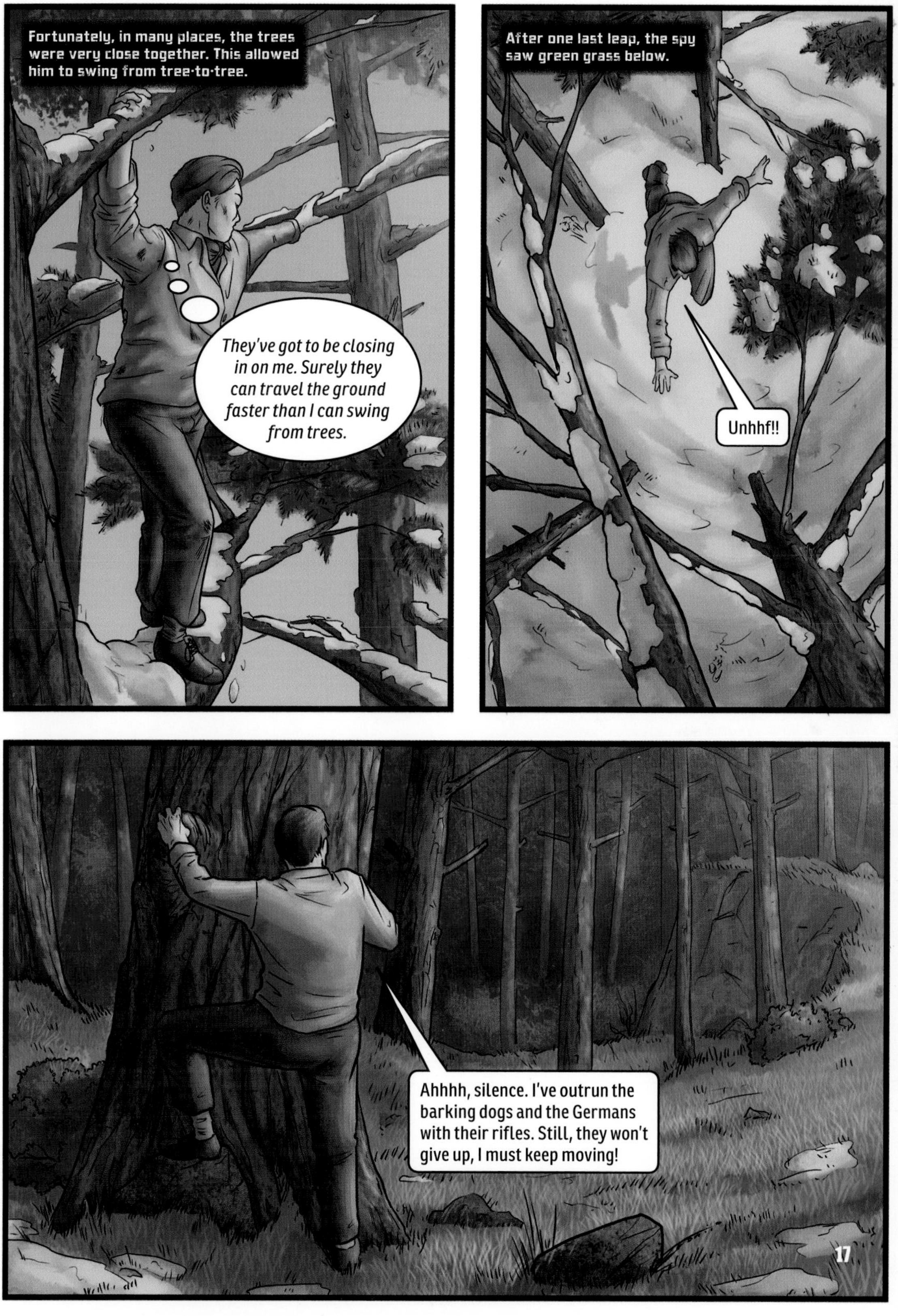
Fortunately, in many places, the trees were very close together. This allowed him to swing from tree-to-tree.
They've got to be closing in on me. Surely they can travel the ground faster than I can swing from trees.
After one last leap, the spy saw green grass below.
Unhhf!!
Ahhhh, silence. I've outrun the barking dogs and the Germans with their rifles. Still, they won't give up, I must keep moving!

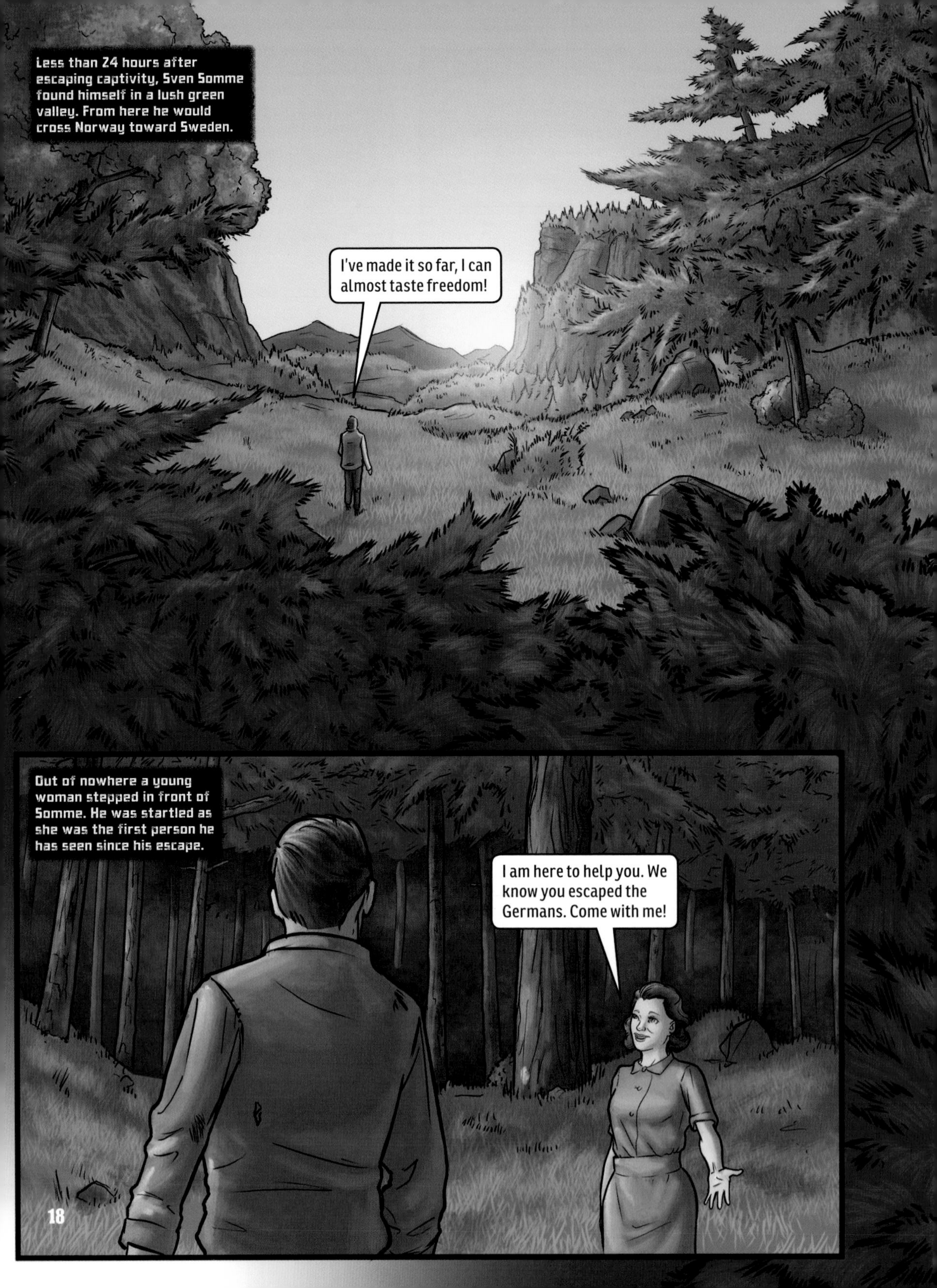
Less than 24 hours after escaping captivity, Sven Somme found himself in a lush green valley. From here he would cross Norway toward Sweden.
I've made it so far, I can almost taste freedom!
Out of nowhere a young woman stepped in front of Somme. He was startled as she was the first person he has seen since his escape.
I am here to help you. We know you escaped the Germans. Come with me!

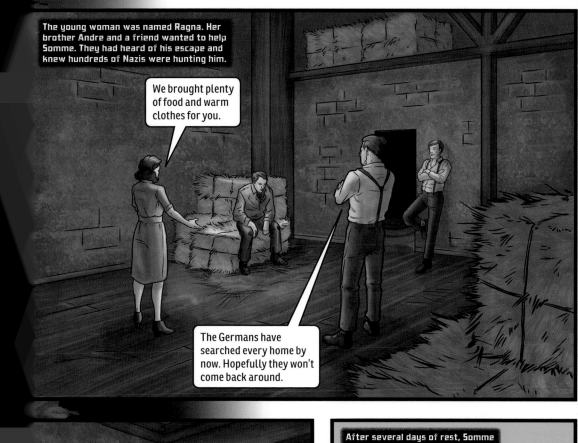

The young woman was named Ragna. Her brother Andre and a friend wanted to help Somme. They had heard of his escape and knew hundreds of Nazis were hunting him.

We brought plenty of food and warm clothes for you.

The Germans have searched every home by now. Hopefully they won't come back around.

You cannot cross the mountains in those shoes. Try my boots to see if they fit.

Thank you. I truly don't know how to repay you.

Make it safely to Sweden and show those Nazis they can't mess with a Norwegian!

After several days of rest, Somme prepared to continue his journey. He began by writing a letter to a member of the resistance.

Kristian, I want a new name, an identity card, a passport, and some money.

He directed the resistance to deliver the supplies to a safe house to the east. It was the next stop on his escape route.

19

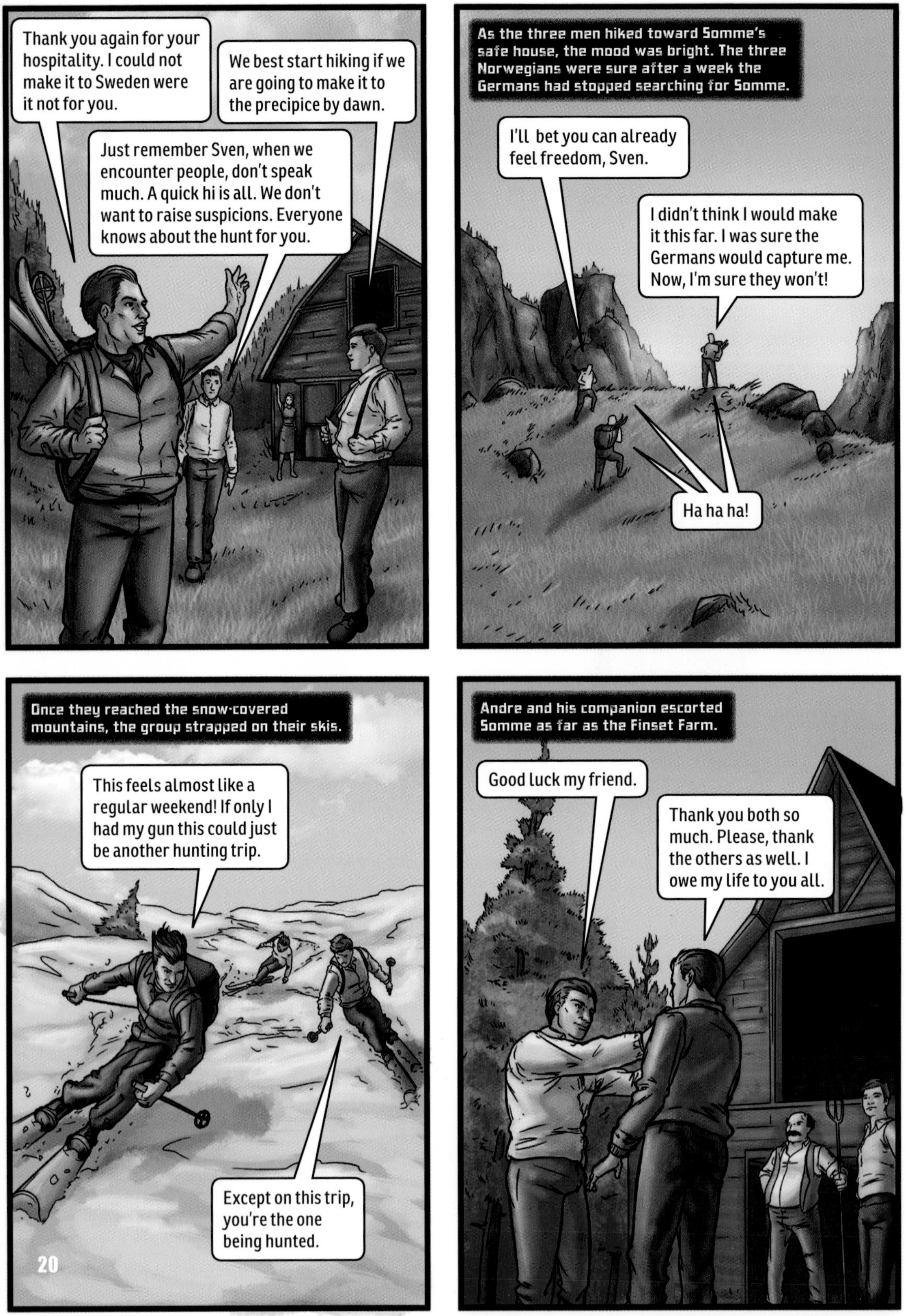
Thank you again for your hospitality. I could not make it to Sweden were it not for you.
We best start hiking if we are going to make it to the precipice by dawn.
Just remember Sven, when we encounter people, don't speak much. A quick hi is all. We don't want to raise suspicions. Everyone knows about the hunt for you.
As the three men hiked toward Somme's safe house, the mood was bright. The three Norwegians were sure after a week the Germans had stopped searching for Somme.
I'll bet you can already feel freedom, Sven.
I didn't think I would make it this far. I was sure the Germans would capture me. Now, I'm sure they won't!
Ha ha ha!
Once they reached the snow-covered mountains, the group strapped on their skis.
This feels almost like a regular weekend! If only I had my gun this could just be another hunting trip.
Except on this trip, you're the one being hunted.
Andre and his companion escorted Somme as far as the Finset Farm.
Good luck my friend.
Thank you both so much. Please, thank the others as well. I owe my life to you all.

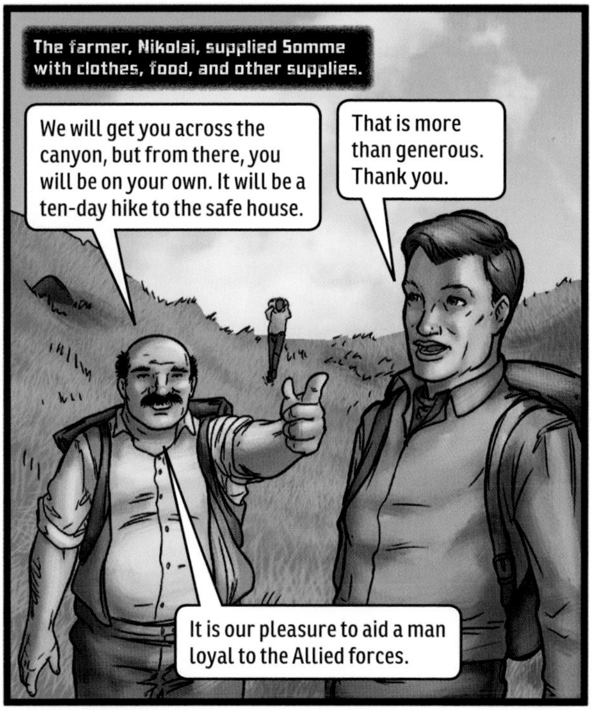
The farmer, Nikolai, supplied Somme with clothes, food, and other supplies.
We will get you across the canyon, but from there, you will be on your own. It will be a ten-day hike to the safe house.
That is more than generous. Thank you.
It is our pleasure to aid a man loyal to the Allied forces.

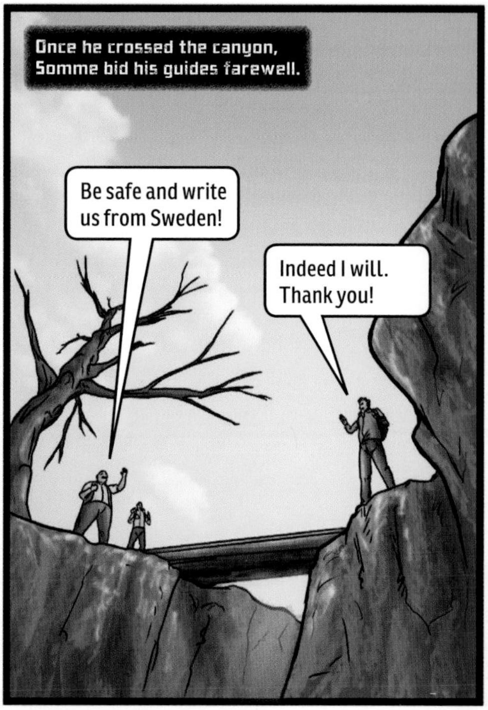
Once he crossed the canyon, Somme bid his guides farewell.
Be safe and write us from Sweden!
Indeed I will. Thank you!

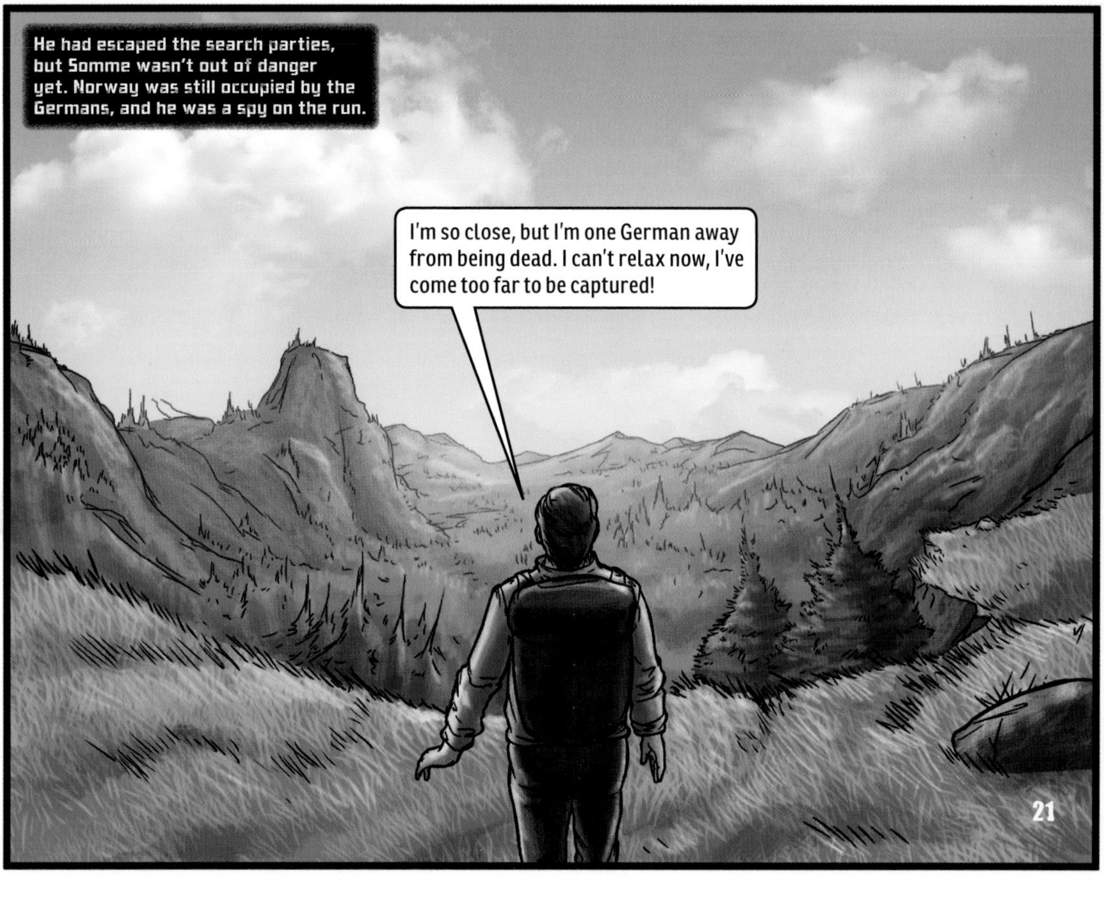
He had escaped the search parties, but Somme wasn't out of danger yet. Norway was still occupied by the Germans, and he was a spy on the run.
I'm so close, but I'm one German away from being dead. I can't relax now, I've come too far to be captured!

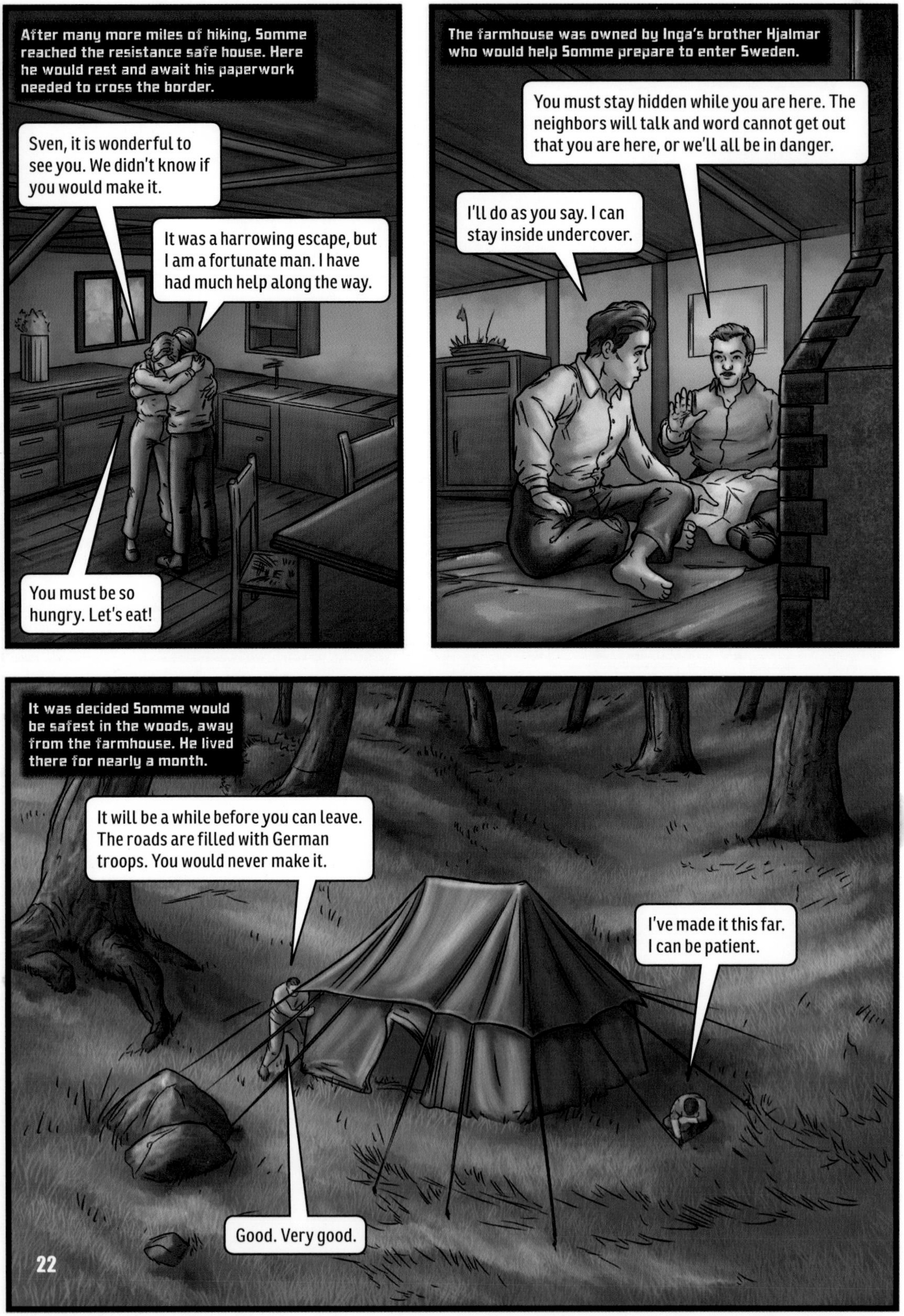
After many more miles of hiking, Somme reached the resistance safe house. Here he would rest and await his paperwork needed to cross the border.
Sven, it is wonderful to see you. We didn't know if you would make it.
It was a harrowing escape, but I am a fortunate man. I have had much help along the way.
You must be so hungry. Let's eat!
The farmhouse was owned by Inga's brother Hjalmar who would help Somme prepare to enter Sweden.
You must stay hidden while you are here. The neighbors will talk and word cannot get out that you are here, or we'll all be in danger.
I'll do as you say. I can stay inside undercover.
It was decided Somme would be safest in the woods, away from the farmhouse. He lived there for nearly a month.
It will be a while before you can leave. The roads are filled with German troops. You would never make it.
I've made it this far. I can be patient.
Good. Very good.

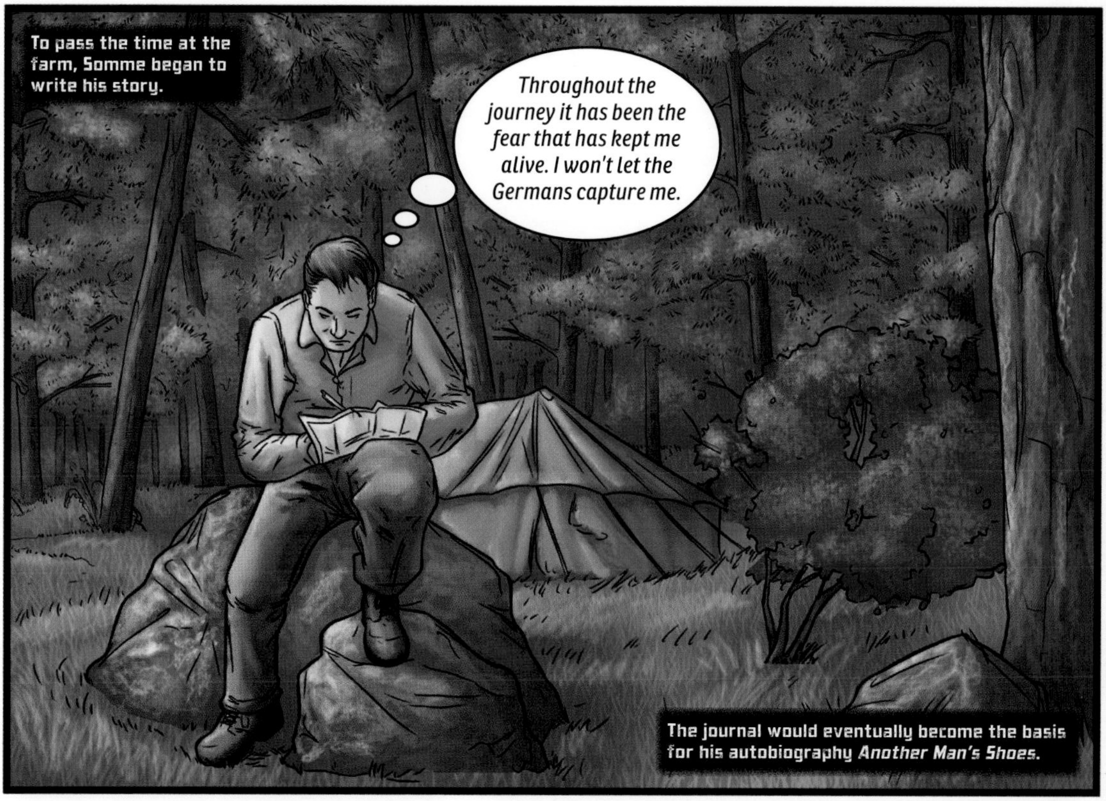
To pass the time at the farm, Somme began to write his story.
Throughout the journey it has been the fear that has kept me alive. I won't let the Germans capture me.
The journal would eventually become the basis for his autobiography *Another Man's Shoes*.

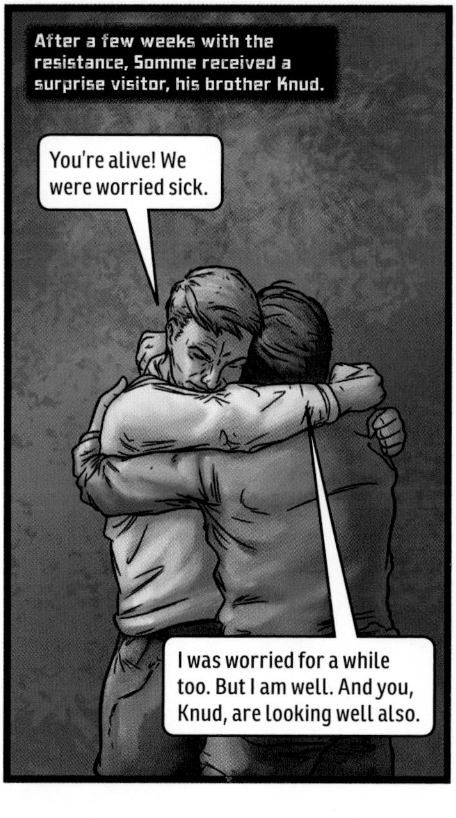
After a few weeks with the resistance, Somme received a surprise visitor, his brother Knud.
You're alive! We were worried sick.
I was worried for a while too. But I am well. And you, Knud, are looking well also.

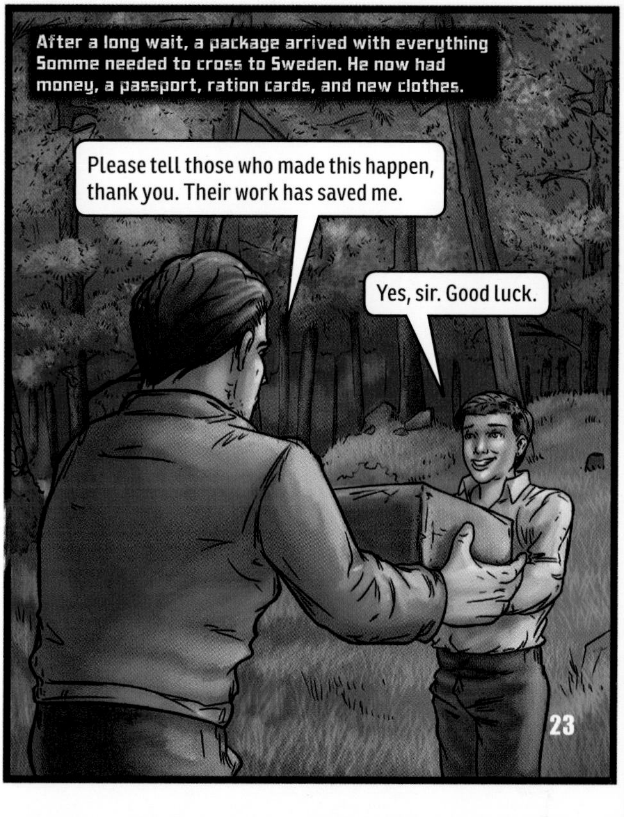
After a long wait, a package arrived with everything Somme needed to cross to Sweden. He now had money, a passport, ration cards, and new clothes.
Please tell those who made this happen, thank you. Their work has saved me.
Yes, sir. Good luck.

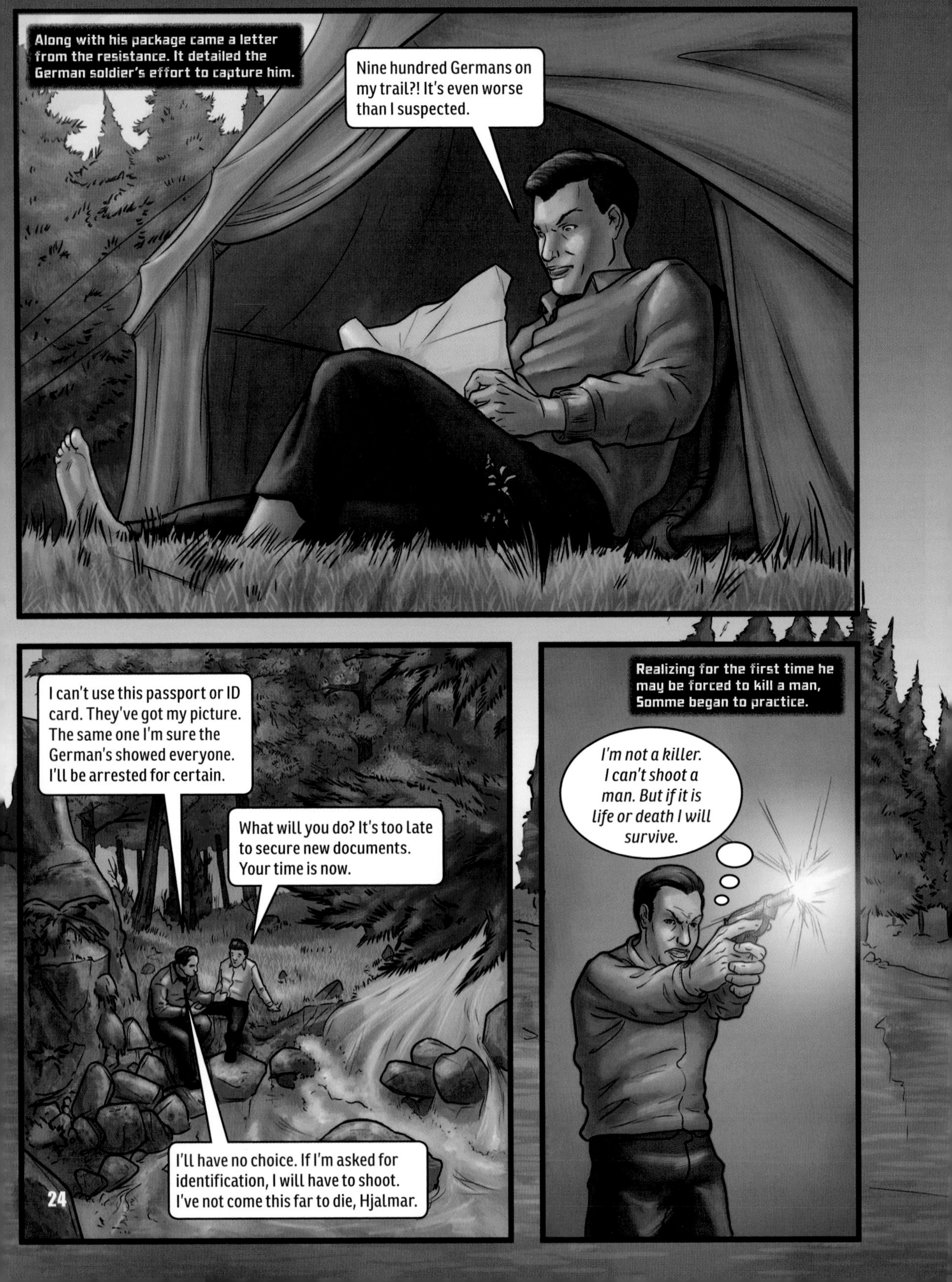
Along with his package came a letter from the resistance. It detailed the German soldier's effort to capture him.
Nine hundred Germans on my trail?! It's even worse than I suspected.
I can't use this passport or ID card. They've got my picture. The same one I'm sure the German's showed everyone. I'll be arrested for certain.
What will you do? It's too late to secure new documents. Your time is now.
I'll have no choice. If I'm asked for identification, I will have to shoot. I've not come this far to die, Hjalmar.
Realizing for the first time he may be forced to kill a man, Somme began to practice.
I'm not a killer. I can't shoot a man. But if it is life or death I will survive.

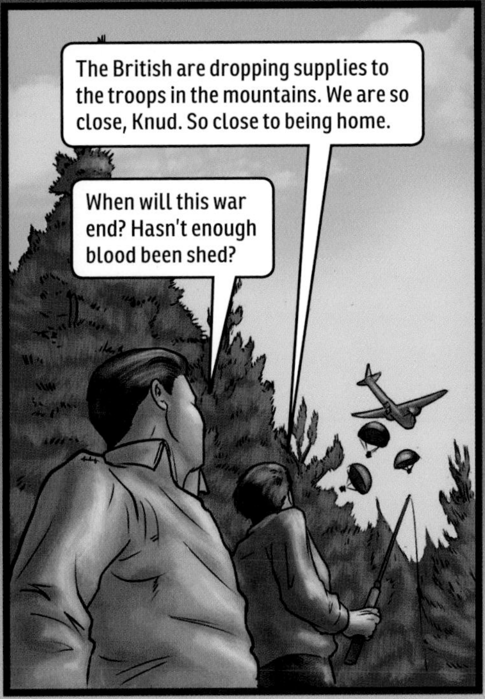
The British are dropping supplies to the troops in the mountains. We are so close, Knud. So close to being home.
When will this war end? Hasn't enough blood been shed?

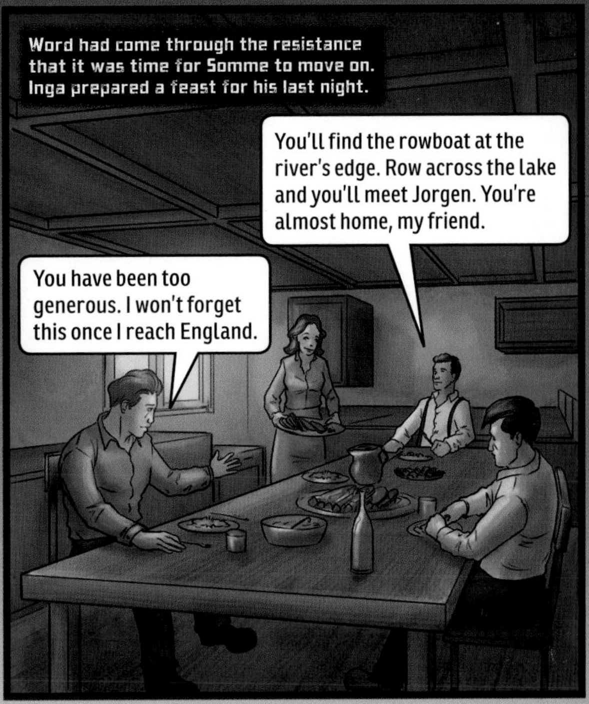
Word had come through the resistance that it was time for Somme to move on. Inga prepared a feast for his last night.
You'll find the rowboat at the river's edge. Row across the lake and you'll meet Jorgen. You're almost home, my friend.
You have been too generous. I won't forget this once I reach England.

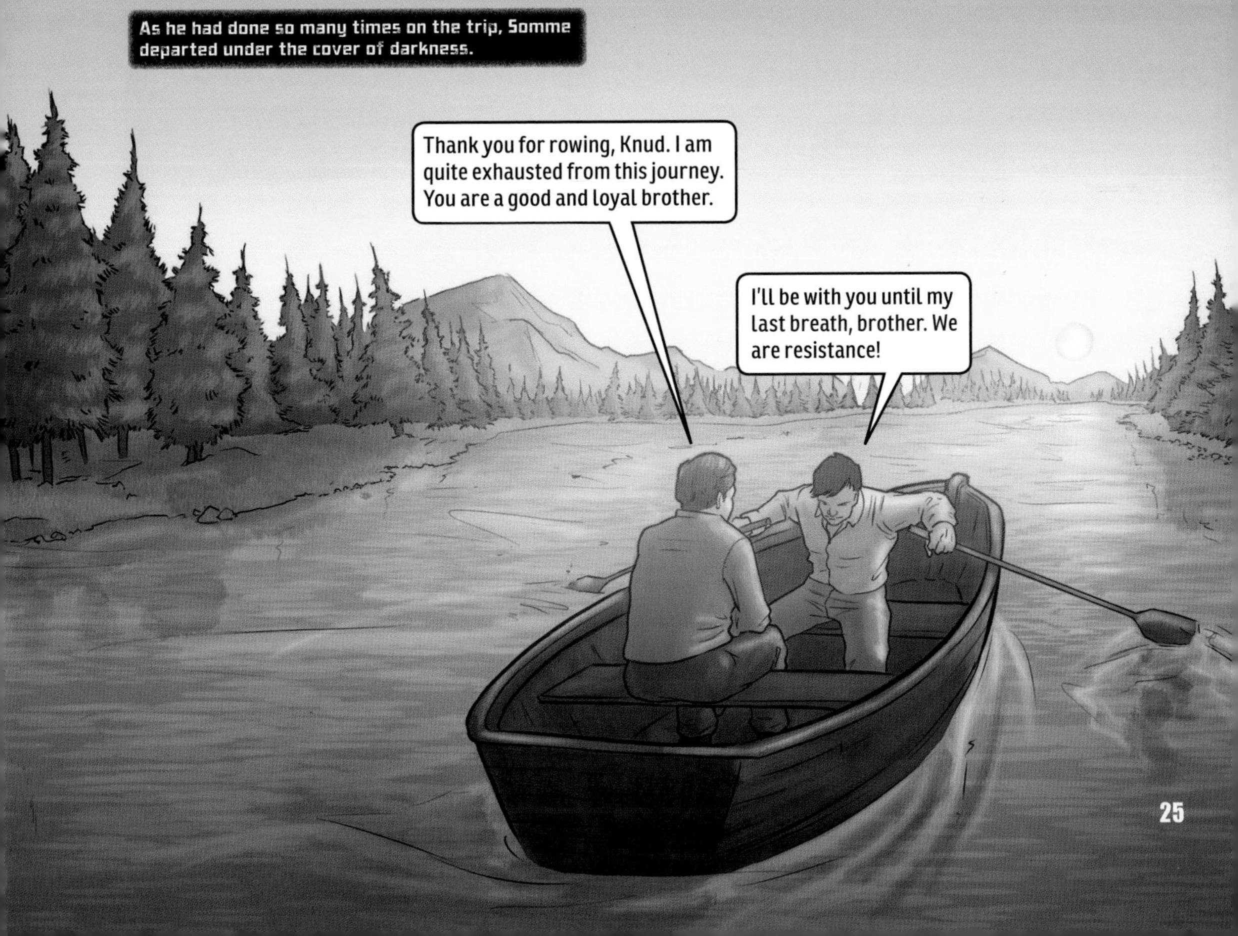
As he had done so many times on the trip, Somme departed under the cover of darkness.
Thank you for rowing, Knud. I am quite exhausted from this journey. You are a good and loyal brother.
I'll be with you until my last breath, brother. We are resistance!

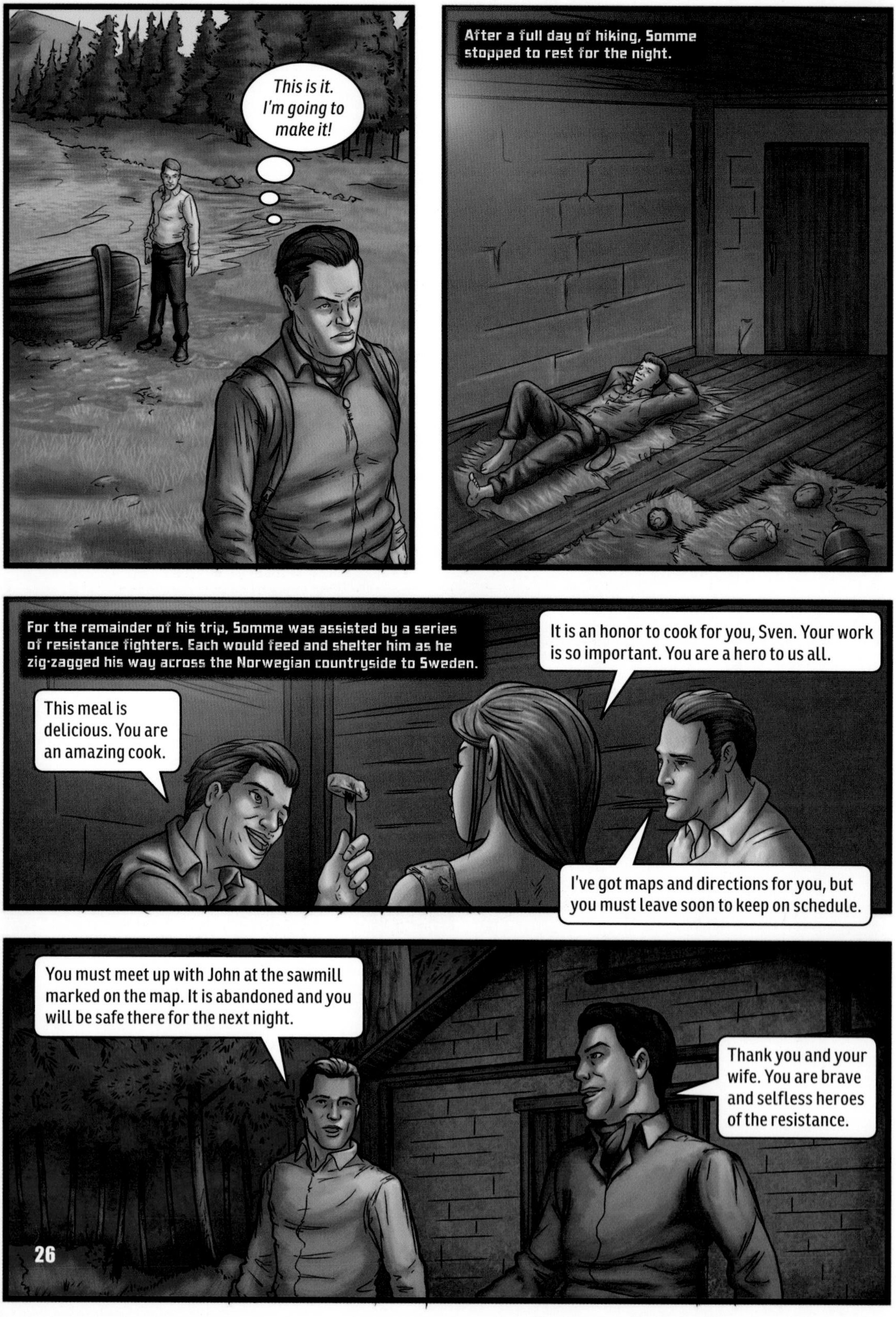
This is it. I'm going to make it!
After a full day of hiking, Somme stopped to rest for the night.
For the remainder of his trip, Somme was assisted by a series of resistance fighters. Each would feed and shelter him as he zig-zagged his way across the Norwegian countryside to Sweden.
This meal is delicious. You are an amazing cook.
It is an honor to cook for you, Sven. Your work is so important. You are a hero to us all.
I've got maps and directions for you, but you must leave soon to keep on schedule.
You must meet up with John at the sawmill marked on the map. It is abandoned and you will be safe there for the next night.
Thank you and your wife. You are brave and selfless heroes of the resistance.

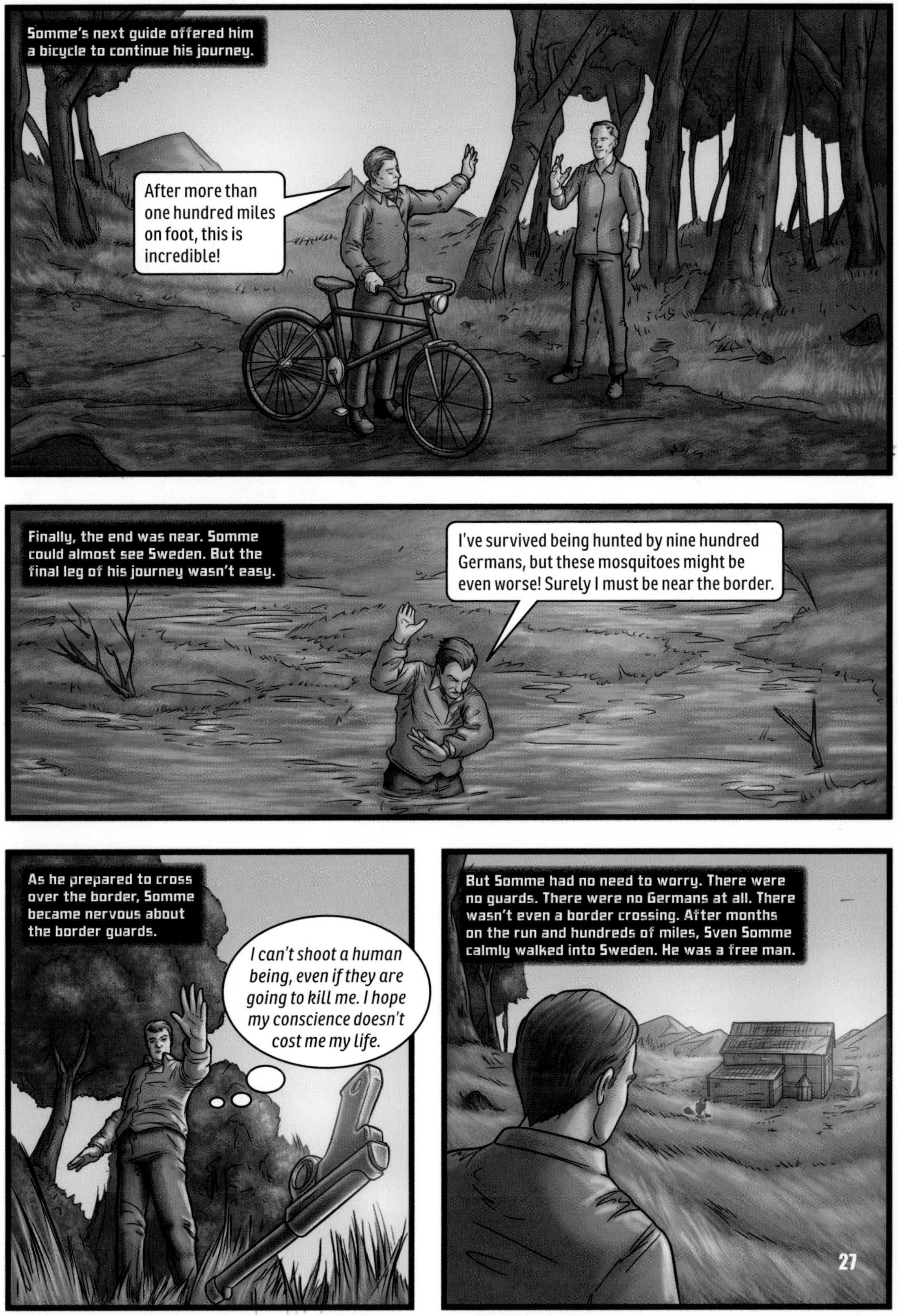
Somme's next guide offered him a bicycle to continue his journey.
After more than one hundred miles on foot, this is incredible!
Finally, the end was near. Somme could almost see Sweden. But the final leg of his journey wasn't easy.
I've survived being hunted by nine hundred Germans, but these mosquitoes might be even worse! Surely I must be near the border.
As he prepared to cross over the border, Somme became nervous about the border guards.
I can't shoot a human being, even if they are going to kill me. I hope my conscience doesn't cost me my life.
But Somme had no need to worry. There were no guards. There were no Germans at all. There wasn't even a border crossing. After months on the run and hundreds of miles, Sven Somme calmly walked into Sweden. He was a free man.

HOME AND FREE

S ven Somme had no idea when he reached Sweden in 1944 that cancer would take his life before his 60th birthday. The man who had outwitted and outrun the Nazi's only had 17 years of freedom to enjoy. And enjoy it he did. After reaching Sweden, Somme was granted asylum, and he returned to London. There he was given a private meeting with the King of Norway, King Haakon, who was living in exile. Somme shared his experiences escaping the Nazis with the King. Settling in England, Somme married his British wife, Primrose. Together they had three children, all daughters. Somme wrote a book detailing his life as a spy for the resistance. *Another Man's Shoes* told the story of his capture and escape in great detail. It became his legacy following his death in 1961.

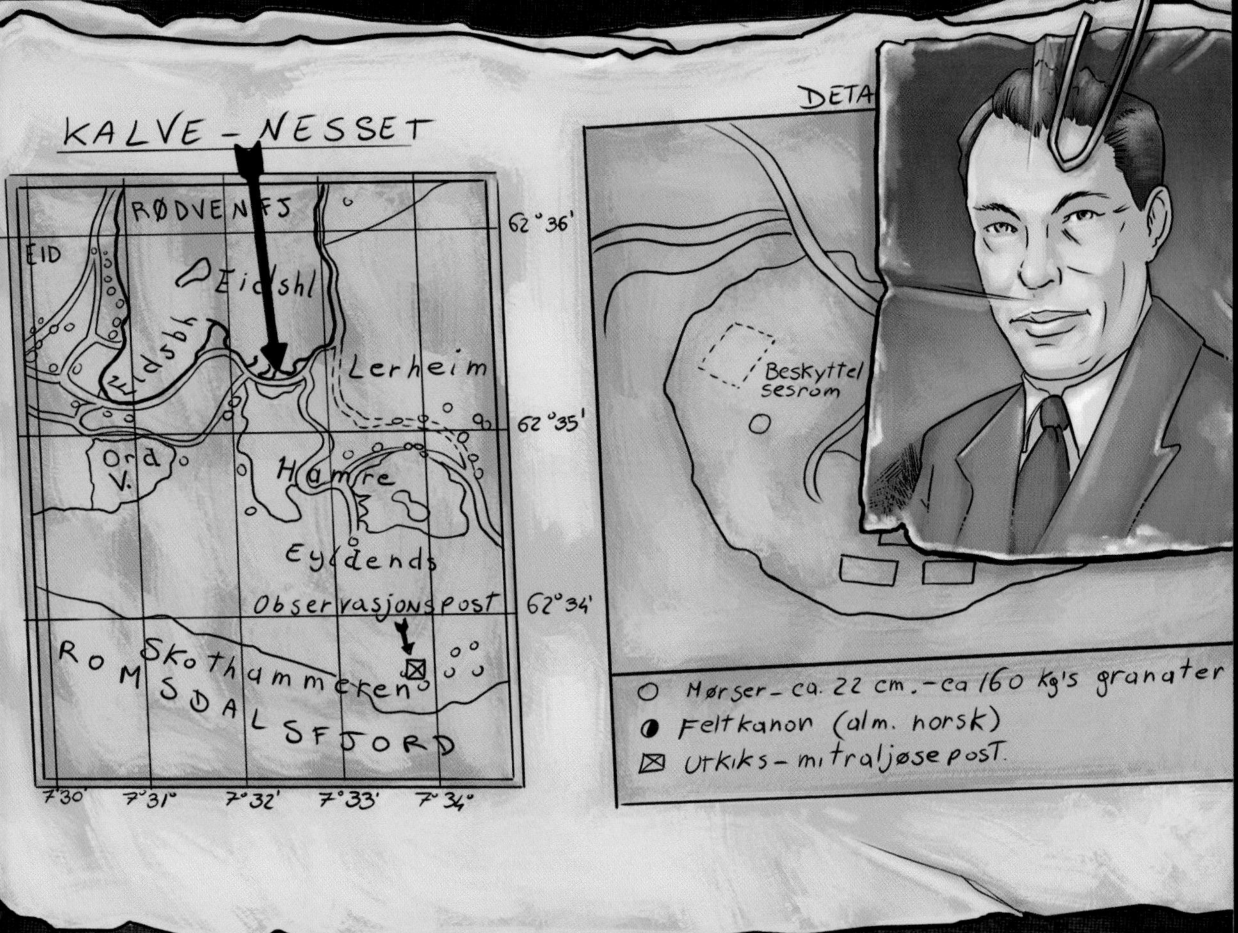
KALVE-NESSET
RØDVENFJ
EID
Eidshl
Eidsbr
Lerheim
62°36'
62°35'
62°34'
Ord V.
Hamre
Eyldends
Observasjonspost
ROMSDALSFJORD
Skothammeren
7°30'
7°31'
7°32'
7°33'
7°34'
DETA
Beskyttelsesrom
Mørser – ca. 22 cm. – ca 160 kg's granater
Feltkanon (alm. norsk)
Utkiks-mitraljøsepost.

Decades later, one of Somme's daughters, Ellie, was cleaning out her mom's residence when she came upon a box. Inside she found letters, maps and other materials Somme had kept from his days as a spy for the resistance. For Ellie, and the rest of Somme's family, it confirmed what they already knew. Sven Somme was a man who risked his life to free his country and protect the world. He was a hero.

GLOSSARY

Allied forces (AL-lyd FORSS-ess)—countries united against Germany during World War II, including France, the United States, Canada, Great Britain, and others

Axis powers (AK-sis POU-urs)—a group of countries that fought together in World War II; the Axis powers included Japan, Italy, and Germany

contraband (KON-truh-band)—anything a person has that is against the law to possess

detain (duh-TAYN)—to hold prisoner

Gestapo (guh-STAH-poh)—the secret police of Nazi Germany

Nazi (NOT-see)—a member of the National Socialist Party led by Adolf Hitler that controlled Germany before and during World War II

precipice (PRESS-uh-pis)—a cliff with an overhanging face

resistance (ri-ZISS-tuhnss)—a secret group of fighters that work against authority, especially in an occupied country

safe house (SAYF HOUSS)—a place where spies or other secret agents can go for help and protection

trespass (TRESS-pass)—to enter someone's private property without permission

zoologist (zoh-OL-uh-jist)—a person who specializes in working with animals

CRITICAL THINKING
USING THE COMMON CORE

1. What is the significance of the title for Somme's autobiography? Explain using details from the text to support your answer.

2. Considering his journey through the snow-covered forest, what would be another possibility for the title? Use details from the text to support your answer.

3. Even though Somme was a soldier, the reader will notice that he doesn't seem to be perfectly suited for that job. How do we know this? Use details from the text to support your answer.

READ MORE

Burgan, Michael. *World War II Pilots.* You Choose Books: World War II. North Mankato, Minn.: Capstone Press, 2013.

Mitchell, Susan K. *Spies and Lies: Famous and Infamous Spies.* The Secret World of Spies. Berkeley Heighys, N.J.: Enslow Publishing, 2012.

Price, Sean Stewart. *World War II Spies.* Classified. North Mankato, Minn.: Capstone Press 2014.

INTERNET SITES

FactHound offers a safe, fun way to find Internet sites related to this book. All sites on FactHound have been researched by our staff.

Here's all you do:

Visit *www.facthound.com*

Type in this code: 9781515735298

 Check out projects, games and lots more at **www.capstonekids.com**

INDEX

TITLES IN THIS SET

BEHIND ENEMY LINES:
The Escape of Robert Grimes with the Comet Line

DEATH CAMP UPRISING:
The Escape from Sobibor Concentration Camp

OUTRUNNING THE NAZIS:
The Brave Escape of Resistance Fighter Sven Somme

TUNNELING TO FREEDOM:
The Great Escape from Stalag Luft III